# What are the Branches of Democracy?

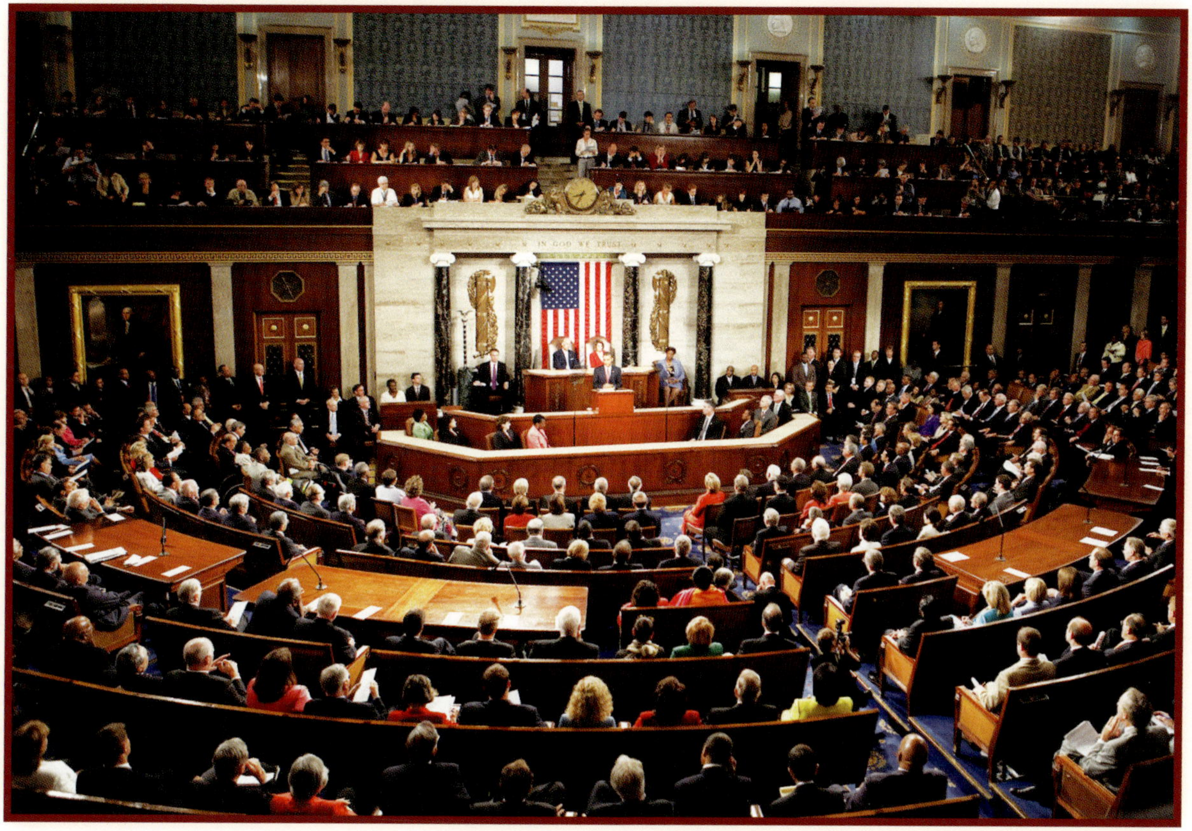

Ann H. Matzke

rourkeeducationalmedia.com

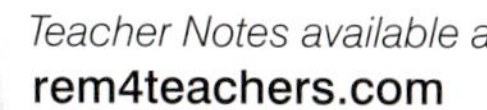

www.rourkeeducationalmedia.com

PHOTO CREDITS: Cover: © t_kimura, Diana Walters, Alan Crosthwaite; Title Page, Page 11: © Lawrence Jackson; Page 3: © GYI NSEA; Page 4: © Library of Congress; Page 5: © Royce DeGrie; Page 6: © Shane Obrien, iconeer; Page 7: © iconeer; Page 8, 12, 13, 17, 18, 19: © AP Images; Page 9: © Jeremy Edwards; Page 10: © U.S. Senate, 111th Congress, Senate Photo Studio; Page 14: © Wikipedia; Page 15: © WilliamSherman; Page 16: © ihsanyildizli; Page 20, 21: © Gene Chutka;

Edited by: Precious McKenzie
Cover design by: Tara Raymo
Interior design by: Renee Brady

**Library of Congress PCN Data**

What are the Branches of Democracy?/Ann H. Matzke
(Little World Social Studies)
ISBN 978-1-61810-146-4(hard cover)(alk. paper)
ISBN 978-1-61810-279-9(soft cover)
Library of Congress Control Number: 2011945873

Rourke Educational Media
Printed in the United States of America

rourkeeducationalmedia.com
customerservice@rourkeeducationalmedia.com • PO Box 643328 Vero Beach, Florida 32964

In the United States, we **elect** people to run our government and make our **laws**. This type of government is called a democracy.

The Constitution sets the rules for our government and explains **rights** and freedoms.

George Washington was a delegate to the Continental Congress.

## Democracy Fact

In 1787, fifty-five delegates called the Continental Congress, met to write the U.S. Constitution.

The Constitution divides our government into three parts, or branches.

# Three Branches of the Government

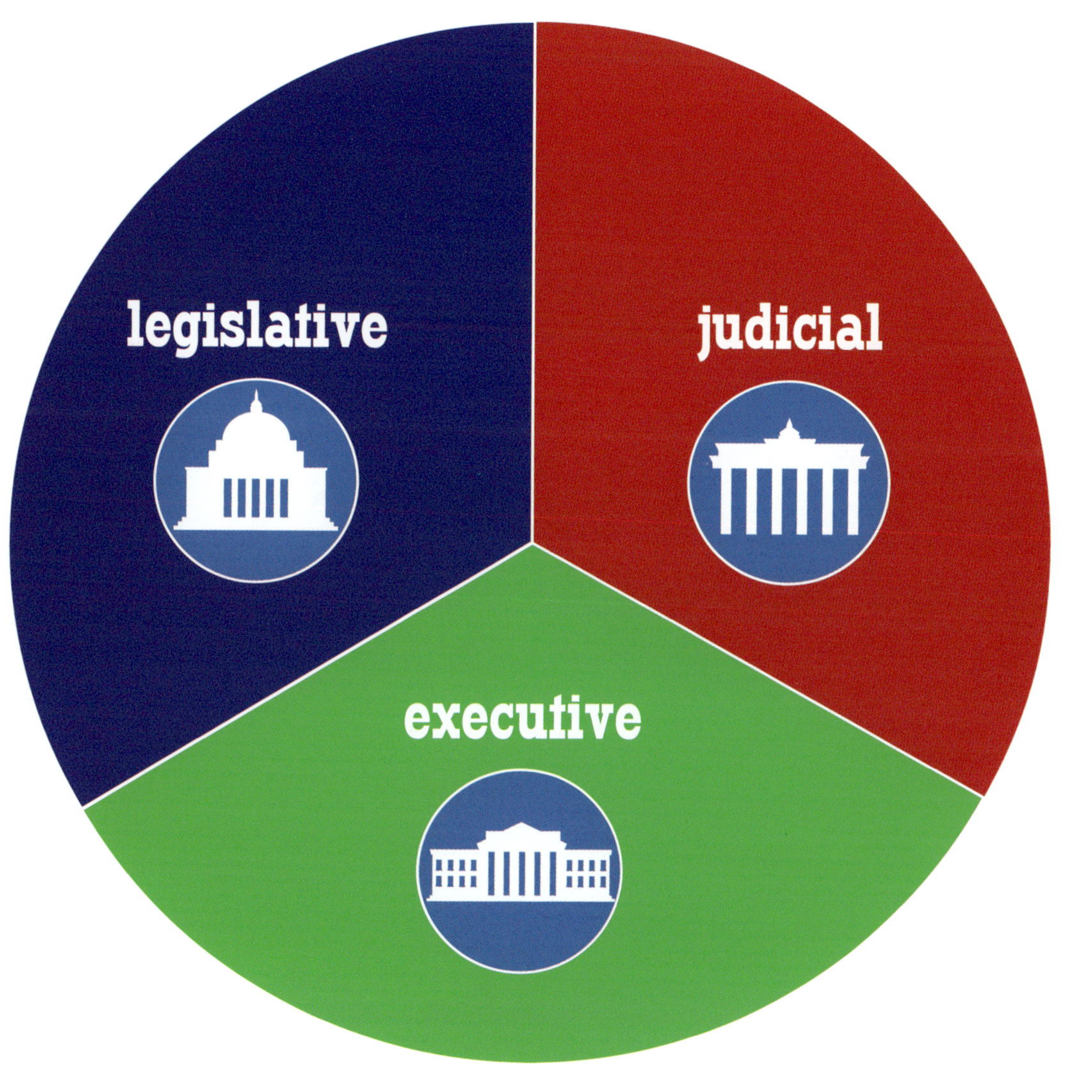

Congress is the legislative branch that makes the laws.

The United States Congress

The Congress gathers in the Capitol building to make the laws for the nation.

Congress is divided into the Senate and the House of Representatives. Each group helps to write and vote on the laws.

The United States Senate

The United States House of Representatives

## Democracy Fact

In the United States there are 435 Representatives in the House of Representatives and 100 Senators in the Senate. Representatives are determined by population. But each state has just 2 Senators.

## Democracy Fact

A presidential election is held every four years in November. A president may be re-elected for a second term.

The president is the leader of the executive branch and he approves the laws.

The president is in charge of the **armed forces**, which keep our country safe.

Army

Navy

Air Force

Marine Corps

Coast Guard

## Democracy Fact

The armed forces include: the Army, Navy, Air Force, Marine Corps, and Coast Guard.

Our **court system** is part of the judicial branch which makes sure the laws are correct and used fairly.

**The United States Supreme Courthouse**

## Democracy Fact

Few cases reach the highest court. The Supreme Court has nine judges called Justices.

## Democracy Fact

When Congress passes a new law the president must approve it.

Each branch is a part of a system of checks and balances so no branch has too much power.

Our three branches of government protect our rights as free people of the United States.

Lincoln Memorial, Washington D.C.

# Picture Glossary

**armed forces** (armed forss-is): The different types of military that serve our country.

**court** (kort): Place where legal cases are heard and decided.

**elect** (i-LEKT): To choose someone or decide something by voting.

**laws** (lawz): Rules made by the government that must be obeyed.

**rights** (rites): Something the law says you can have or do.

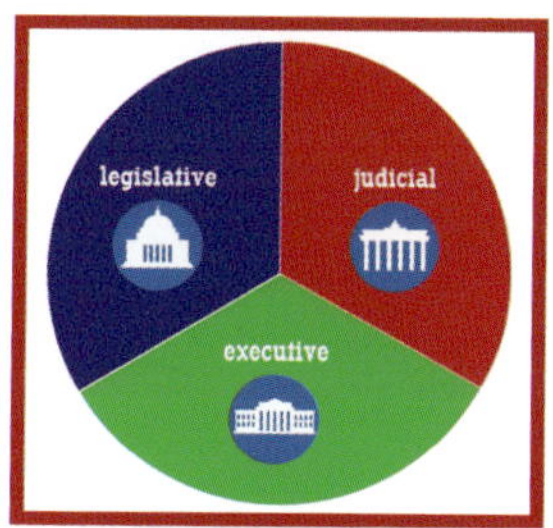


**system** (SISS-tuhm): Orderly way of doing something.

# Index



## Websites

pbskids.org/democracy/govandme/

kids.clerk.house.gov/

www.congressforkids.net/

## About the Author

Ann H. Matzke is a children's librarian. She has an MFA in Writing for children and young adults from Hamline University. Ann lives with her family in Gothenburg, Nebraska. Nebraska is the only state to have a one-house legislature called a Unicameral. Ann enjoys traveling, reading, and writing books for children.